ATHENS

The Glorious City

Athens, the capital of Greece, boasts a rich and storied history that spans millennia. Its origins can be traced back over 3,400 years to the ancient Mycenaean civilization. However, it truly rose to prominence during the Golden Age of Athens in the 5th century BC, under the leadership of statesman Pericles. This period witnessed remarkable achievements in philosophy, art, and democracy, with luminaries like Socrates, Plato, and Aristotle shaping Western thought.

Athens later fell under Roman and Byzantine rule, enduring periods of decline and resurgence. In the modern era, it played a pivotal role in the Greek War of Independence and eventually became the capital of Greece in 1834. Today, Athens stands as a vibrant metropolis, blending its rich history with contemporary culture, offering a kaleidoscope of experiences for residents and visitors alike.

The Acropolis is a historic hilltop citadel crowned by ancient architectural marvels, including the iconic Parthenon. It's a symbol of Greek civilization's enduring legacy and stands as a UNESCO World Heritage Site, drawing visitors from around the world to marvel at its ancient beauty and significance.

The Parthenon is an iconic ancient temple located on the Acropolis hill. This architectural masterpiece is dedicated to the goddess Athena and is renowned for its Doric columns and intricate sculptures. It is a symbol of classical Greek art and culture, and its enduring legacy continues to inspire visitors and scholars worldwide.

The Acropolis Museum is a modern architectural marvel that houses a remarkable collection of ancient Greek artifacts and sculptures. Designed to complement the historic Acropolis site, the museum offers a fascinating journey through Greece's rich cultural heritage, showcasing archaeological treasures from the Parthenon and other ancient structures. It provides visitors with an immersive experience, making it a must-visit destination for those seeking to explore the wonders of classical Athens.

———————————————→

The Plaka District is a charming and picturesque neighborhood nestled beneath the Acropolis. Known for its narrow winding streets, neoclassical architecture, and vibrant atmosphere, it offers a delightful blend of historic charm and modern vitality. Visitors can explore quaint shops, savor traditional Greek cuisine, and soak in the unique ambiance of this iconic Athenian district.

#5
Ancient Agora

———————————————→

The Ancient Agora is a historic gathering place that served as the heart of the city's political and social life in antiquity. It features well-preserved ruins, including the Stoa of Attalos and the Temple of Hephaestus, offering a glimpse into ancient Greek democracy and daily life. This archaeological site is a captivating window into the past, where visitors can explore the remnants of an ancient civic center that played a pivotal role in shaping Western civilization.

Temple of Olympian Zeus

⟶

The Temple of Olympian Zeus is a colossal ancient temple dedicated to the king of the Greek gods, Zeus. It once housed one of the largest cult statues in the ancient world and is a testament to the grandeur of ancient Greek architecture. Today, its towering columns and archaeological remains stand as a majestic reminder of the city's rich history and the reverence the Greeks had for their gods.

National Archaeological Museum

→

The National Archaeological Museum is a renowned institution housing an extensive collection of ancient artifacts. It offers a captivating journey through Greek history, featuring treasures from various periods, including sculptures, pottery, and artifacts from ancient civilizations. This museum is a treasure trove for history enthusiasts, providing insight into the profound cultural and artistic heritage of Greece.

#8
Syntagma Square

→

Syntagma Square is the central and bustling square of the city. It serves as a hub for both locals and tourists, surrounded by key landmarks like the Greek Parliament Building and luxury hotels. With its vibrant atmosphere, it's a gathering place for events, protests, and celebrations, making it a dynamic focal point of Athenian life.

→

Ermou Street is a vibrant and bustling shopping avenue. It is lined with a wide variety of stores, from high-end boutiques to popular retail chains, making it a prime destination for fashion enthusiasts and shoppers. This pedestrian-friendly street offers a delightful blend of modern shopping experiences against the backdrop of Athens' historic charm.

#10
Monastiraki Square

→

Monastiraki Square is a lively and historic area located in the heart of the city. It's known for its vibrant flea market, where visitors can discover an array of antiques, souvenirs, and unique items. This bustling square also offers a mix of traditional tavernas, cafes, and a picturesque view of the Acropolis, making it a captivating spot for both shopping and cultural experiences in Athens.

————————————————→

The Benaki Museum is a prominent cultural institution dedicated to showcasing Greek art and history. It features a diverse collection of artifacts, from ancient to contemporary, providing insight into Greece's rich cultural heritage. This museum is a must-visit for those seeking to explore the multifaceted aspects of Greek civilization through its remarkable exhibits and displays.

#12
National Garden of Athens

→

The National Garden of Athens is a tranquil oasis in the heart of the city. This lush green space offers a peaceful retreat from the urban hustle and bustle, with winding paths, serene ponds, and diverse plant life. It's a favorite spot for both locals and visitors to relax, stroll, and enjoy the natural beauty amid the historical surroundings of Athens.

→

Lycabettus Hill is an iconic natural landmark that offers panoramic views of the city. This steep hill is a popular destination for hikers and visitors seeking breathtaking vistas of Athens and the Aegean Sea. Atop Lycabettus, there is a chapel and a restaurant, making it a picturesque spot for both daytime excursions and evening dining with a view.

#14
Panathenaic Stadium

→

The Panathenaic Stadium is a historic athletic arena often referred to as the "Kallimarmaro Stadium." It is renowned for its stunning white marble construction and its role in hosting the first modern Olympic Games in 1896. This ancient stadium is a symbol of the Olympic spirit and continues to host events and ceremonies, offering visitors a chance to step into the rich history of athletic competition in Greece.

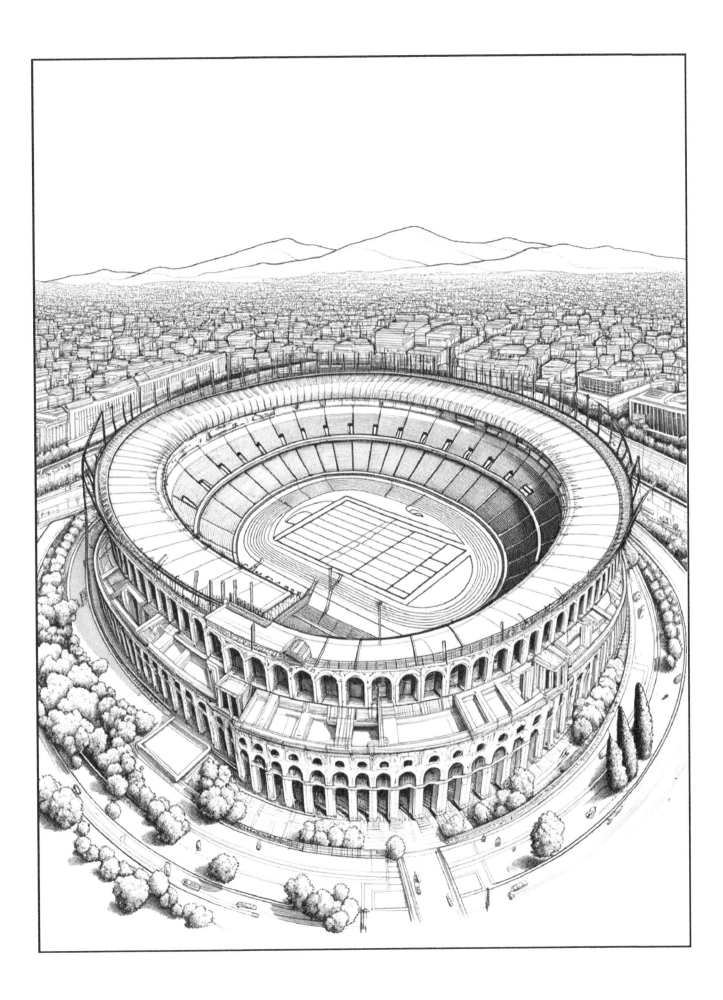

Odeon of Herodes Atticus

-->

The Odeon of Herodes Atticus is a magnificent ancient amphitheater located on the southern slope of the Acropolis. This open-air theater, built in the 2nd century AD, is renowned for its exceptional acoustics and hosts a variety of cultural performances, including concerts and classical plays. It provides a captivating setting where visitors can enjoy artistic and musical events while immersed in the historic ambiance of Athens.

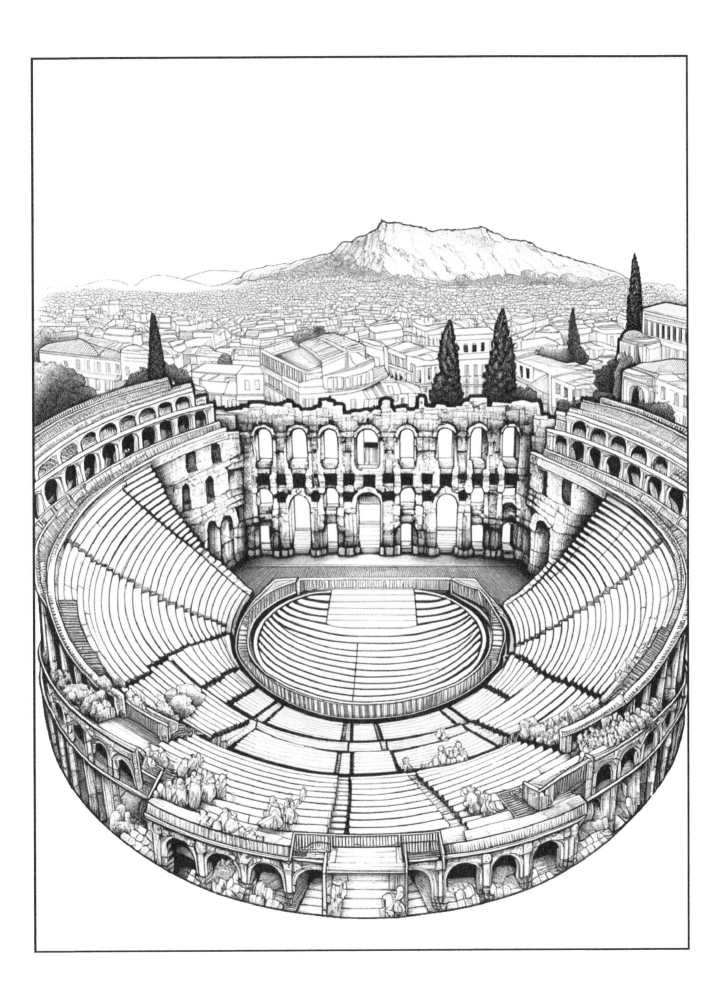

Kerameikos Archaeological Site

→

The Kerameikos Archaeological Site is a significant historical site that once served as the city's ancient burial grounds and an important residential and industrial district. It features well-preserved ruins, including ancient walls, tombs, and artifacts, offering a glimpse into everyday life in ancient Athens. This archaeological site is a window into the city's past, revealing its cultural and historical heritage through the remains of centuries-old structures and burial sites.

Stavros Niarchos Foundation Cultural Center

→

It is a modern cultural complex that combines art, education, and entertainment. It houses the Greek National Opera and the National Library of Greece, along with beautiful landscaped gardens and a stunning view of the Mediterranean Sea. This state-of-the-art center serves as a hub for cultural activities, performances, and public events, enriching the cultural fabric of Athens and offering a contemporary space for artistic and intellectual pursuits.

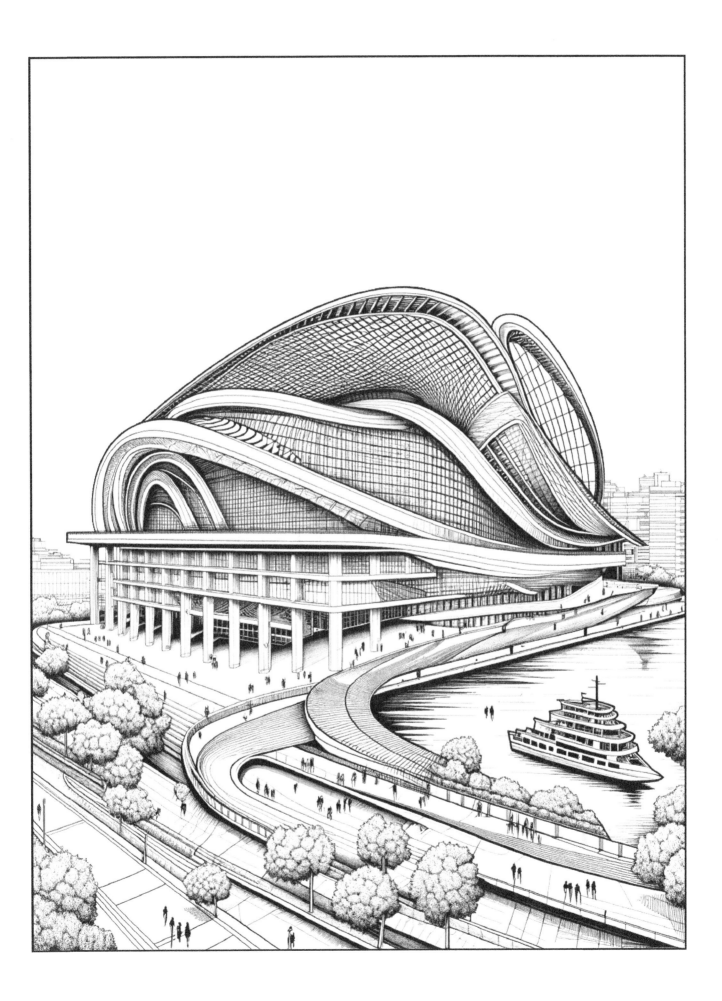

———————————————————→

Anafiotika is a charming and picturesque neighborhood tucked beneath the Acropolis. It resembles a Greek island village with its whitewashed buildings, narrow alleyways, and vibrant flowers, offering a tranquil escape from the bustling city. This unique enclave invites visitors to wander its labyrinthine streets and experience a taste of the Greek islands in the heart of Athens.

National Historical Museum

→

The National Historical Museum is a prominent institution dedicated to preserving and showcasing Greece's rich historical heritage. It features an extensive collection of artifacts, documents, and exhibitions that chronicle the nation's history from ancient times to modern days. This museum is a vital resource for those seeking a comprehensive understanding of Greece's past, offering a compelling journey through its political, cultural, and social evolution over the centuries.

#20
Museum of Cycladic Art

———————————→

The Museum of Cycladic Art is a renowned cultural institution specializing in the art and artifacts of the Cycladic civilization. It houses a remarkable collection of ancient sculptures, pottery, and artifacts from the Cyclades islands, providing valuable insights into the artistic and cultural achievements of this ancient Aegean culture. This museum is a must-visit for those interested in the artistic legacy of the Cyclades, offering a glimpse into the beauty and creativity of ancient Greece.

Byzantine and Christian Museum

---------------------------------→

The Byzantine and Christian Museum is a notable institution dedicated to preserving and showcasing the art and history of the Byzantine Empire and early Christian period. It houses a diverse collection of religious artifacts, icons, mosaics, and manuscripts, providing a comprehensive view of the Byzantine and Christian heritage in Greece. This museum is a valuable resource for those interested in the profound influence of Byzantine art and culture on the region, offering a journey through the spiritual and artistic expressions of the past.

Filopappou Hill is a scenic hilltop offering stunning panoramic views of the city, the Acropolis, and the Saronic Gulf. It is a peaceful and historic site known for its walking trails, ancient ruins, and lush greenery. This hill provides both locals and visitors with a tranquil escape from the urban hustle and an opportunity to immerse themselves in the natural beauty and historical significance of Athens.

Mount Parnitha National Park

→

Mount Parnitha National Park is a pristine natural sanctuary offering hiking trails, lush forests, and diverse wildlife. It provides a serene retreat from the city, where outdoor enthusiasts can explore the beautiful Greek wilderness. The park is known for its stunning landscapes and the opportunity to encounter native flora and fauna while enjoying panoramic vistas of the surrounding region.

#24
Athens Concert Hall

→

The Athens Concert Hall, also known as the Megaron, is a prominent cultural venue. It serves as a hub for music, performing arts, and cultural events. The modern architectural design and state-of-the-art facilities make it a premier destination for concerts, theater productions, and exhibitions, providing a vibrant space for artistic and cultural experiences in the heart of Athens.

#25
Kaisariani Monastery

$\longrightarrow$

The Kaisariani Monastery is a historic religious complex nestled in a serene natural setting. Dating back to the 11th century, it features Byzantine architecture, a church, and well-preserved frescoes. This monastery offers a glimpse into the spiritual and architectural heritage of the region and provides a peaceful escape from the urban environment of Athens.

→

Allou! Fun Park is a popular amusement park and entertainment venue that offers a wide range of thrilling rides, games, and attractions for visitors of all ages. It provides a fun-filled experience with roller coasters, carousels, and arcade games, making it a go-to destination for families and thrill-seekers in Athens. This park is a place to enjoy exciting rides and create lasting memories in a lively and vibrant atmosphere.

Pnyx Hill is an iconic historic site known as the birthplace of democracy. It's an open-air meeting place where ancient Athenians gathered to participate in civic affairs and engage in democratic discussions. Today, it offers visitors a chance to connect with the democratic roots of Western civilization while enjoying panoramic views of Athens and the Acropolis.

Church of Kapnikarea

————————————→

The Church of Kapnikarea is a charming and historic Byzantine-era church located in the heart of the city's bustling shopping district. With its unique architecture and beautiful mosaics, it's a peaceful oasis amid the urban hustle and bustle. This church is a cultural and architectural gem, offering a glimpse into Athens' rich history and spiritual heritage.

National Theatre of Greece

→

The National Theatre of Greece is a prestigious cultural institution dedicated to showcasing Greek and international theater productions. It serves as a hub for the performing arts, hosting a wide range of theatrical performances, from classical Greek tragedies to contemporary plays. With its rich history and commitment to the arts, the National Theatre of Greece is a vital part of the country's cultural landscape, offering captivating performances that resonate with audiences from around the world.

#30
Temple of Hephaestus

→

The Temple of Hephaestus is a stunning ancient Greek temple dedicated to the god of craftsmanship and metallurgy, Hephaestus. This remarkably well-preserved Doric temple is located in the Ancient Agora and is celebrated for its elegant architecture and intricate friezes. It stands as a testament to ancient Greek artistry and craftsmanship and is one of the best-preserved classical temples in the world, offering a glimpse into the architectural splendor of ancient Athens.

#31
Lykavittos Theatre

→

The Lykavittos Theatre is an open-air amphitheater located on the slopes of Mount Lycabettus. It serves as a captivating venue for cultural performances, including concerts, plays, and other artistic events. With its unique setting and panoramic views of Athens, it offers a memorable and enchanting experience for attendees, combining both natural beauty and cultural entertainment in the heart of the city.

Kifisia District is an upscale and leafy residential area known for its elegant mansions, lush gardens, and high-end boutiques. It offers a tranquil escape from the urban bustle of Athens and is a favored neighborhood among affluent residents. Kifisia is characterized by its charming streets, parks, and a vibrant cultural scene, making it a sought-after destination for those seeking a refined and peaceful urban lifestyle.

———————————————————→

The Erechtheion is an iconic ancient Greek temple situated on the Acropolis. It is renowned for its distinctive architecture, including the famous Caryatid statues that support its southern porch. Dedicated to both Athena and Poseidon, this historic temple is a masterpiece of classical architecture and serves as a testament to the artistic and religious significance of the Acropolis in ancient Greece.

→

The Theater of Dionysus is an ancient open-air amphitheater situated at the base of the Acropolis. It is considered one of the birthplaces of Greek drama and a venue where classical plays by playwrights like Sophocles and Euripides were first performed. This historic theater, dedicated to the god of wine and theater, Dionysus, holds a prominent place in the history of Greek theater and continues to be a significant archaeological and cultural site in Athens.

The Roman Agora is an ancient marketplace and civic center built during the Roman period. It features well-preserved ruins, including the iconic Tower of the Winds and the Gate of Athena Archegetis. This archaeological site offers a glimpse into daily life in Roman Athens and stands as a testament to the city's rich history and cultural heritage.

Hadrian's Library is an ancient library and cultural center built by Emperor Hadrian in the 2nd century AD. While little remains of the original structure, it was once a hub of scholarship and intellectual activity. This historical site reflects the Roman influence on Athens and its dedication to learning and culture during antiquity.

#37
Areopagus Hill

$\longrightarrow$

Areopagus Hill is an ancient rocky outcrop located northwest of the Acropolis. Historically, it served as a place for judicial and legislative meetings in ancient Athens. Today, it offers visitors a peaceful vantage point to admire the Acropolis and the city of Athens, making it a popular spot for both historical reflection and scenic views.

→

Mount Lycabettus is a prominent hill that provides panoramic views of the city. With its summit reaching 300 meters above sea level, it's one of the highest points in Athens. Visitors can reach the top by hiking or taking a funicular railway, where they can enjoy breathtaking vistas of Athens, especially during sunset. The hill is also home to a charming chapel and a restaurant, making it a popular destination for both tourists and locals seeking scenic beauty and tranquility in the heart of the city.

Psyrri is a vibrant and eclectic neighborhood known for its artistic flair, lively nightlife, and creative spirit. It features a mix of trendy bars, restaurants, and art galleries, making it a popular destination for entertainment and cultural experiences. This dynamic district is a hub for urban culture, where visitors can explore its bohemian atmosphere and enjoy the local music and arts scene.

#40
Athens Skyline

→

The Athens skyline is a captivating blend of ancient and modern architecture. It features iconic landmarks like the Acropolis and the Parthenon, juxtaposed with contemporary buildings and a bustling cityscape. This skyline offers a unique and picturesque view of Athens, showcasing its rich historical heritage alongside its vibrant urban development.

We 🩶 your feedback

We love to receive reviews from our customers. If you had the opportunity to provide a review we would greatly appreciate it. **Thank you!**

⭐ ⭐ ⭐ ⭐ ⭐

Share your thoughts

Scan the QR code below to give us your impressions and stay tuned for new releases:

More similar books?

If you enjoyed the book you may be interested in more similar books. Scan the QR code below to access Charlotte Griffin's Amazon store: